Christianity
in words and pictures

Sarah Thorley
Designed by the author

CONTENTS

WORD LIST

God = the Father, the Son, the Holy Spirit   God is love. Christians believe in one God who is three parts (like a △, which has three sides). God the Father created the world. He is unseen. God the Son is Jesus Christ who was seen and known on earth. God the Holy Spirit is the life of God in the world.

the Bible   the holy book of Christians

the Gospels   the part of the Bible about Jesus; 'gospel' means 'good news'

Palestine   the country where Jesus lived. Part of it is now known as Israel (or 'the Holy Land')

Jews   the people to whom Jesus belonged; they lived in Palestine

Romans   the people who ruled Palestine at the time of Jesus

crucifixion   a Roman punishment; a man was nailed to a wooden cross and left there until he died

miracle   a supernatural event which shows God's power

disciple   a person who follows and learns from someone else

the Devil/Satan   the being who is the power of evil in the world

spirit/soul   the part of you that is not your body or your mind. Christians believe it continues to live after death

Holy Communion/Mass/Eucharist/the Lord's Supper   names for the church service at which bread and wine are received

to preach   to tell or teach people about something believed to be important

to bless   to ask for God's special care and protection for someone or something

pilgrimage   a journey to a holy place

Dates   Christian countries count their years from when Christ was born. The time before that is written as B.C. For example 100 B.C. = 100 years Before Christ. Dates after Jesus's birth are written as A.D. 1989 (A.D. stands for Anno Domini, 'in the year of our Lord').

1

1 Jesus

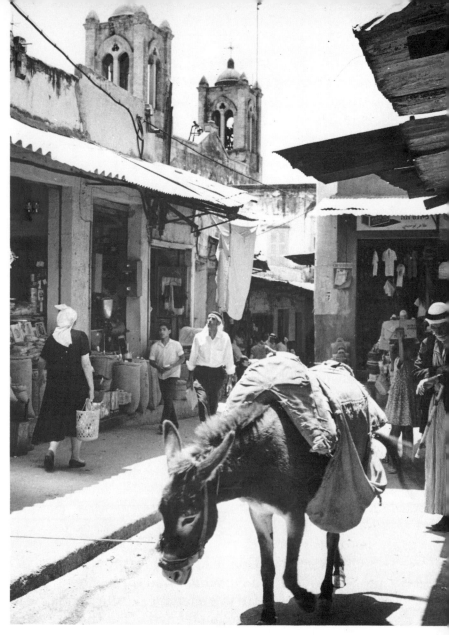

Jesus was a man who lived nearly two thousand years ago. He came from Nazareth, a town in Palestine. This photograph was taken not long ago in Nazareth. The people of Palestine were Jews, so Jesus was born a Jew. Palestine was ruled by the Romans. Jerusalem was the capital city.

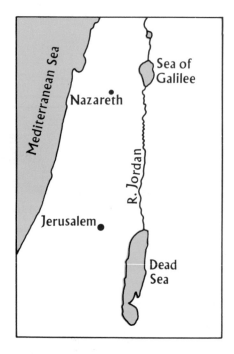

The name Jesus means 'God saves'. Jesus is also known as Jesus Christ. The word Christ is not a surname. It means 'the anointed one'. Messiah has the same meaning. In those days to anoint someone – to mark him with oil – showed that he was special. Kings were anointed. The drawing on the left shows the Jewish king Saul being anointed. For hundreds of years the Jews had been waiting for a Messiah to come from God. He would lead them to freedom from their enemies and show them how to live more godly lives. The Bible says that God's angel came to a young woman called Mary. He told her that she had been chosen to give birth to the promised Messiah. She was to call her baby 'Jesus'.

Christians believe that Jesus was that Messiah. They believe he is God's son. They believe that God became a man on earth and because Jesus was God he did not sin. People of the Jewish faith do not believe that Jesus was the awaited Messiah. Many Jews are still waiting for their true Messiah to come.

All over the world people have made pictures of Jesus but no one knows exactly what he looked like. Here is a copy of one of the first paintings made of him, about 120 years after his death. People in that part of the world have brown skins. Most of the Jews had long hair and beards.

We can read about Jesus in the Bible. He came from the family of a village carpenter. When he grew up he led a very simple life: he had no house, no possessions and no money of his own. He travelled around the country on foot with his twelve disciples (the men he had chosen to help him in his work), telling people about God. As the Jews were expecting a king most of them did not believe that this man could be their Messiah. When Jesus was only thirty-three years old he was killed.

But there were people who had listened carefully to what he had said. They had watched him caring for poor people. They had seen him healing sick people. They had seen him doing things that other human beings could not do; these are called miracles. You can read about them in the Gospels. For three years large crowds followed him. Many people believed that Jesus was God's son, but others were afraid of him and jealous of his power. They plotted against him and crucified him. This picture, taken in Mexico, shows people acting out the story of Jesus's crucifixion. However, death was not the end of Jesus. The greatest miracle was still to come: he came back to life. His closest friends saw him alive several times after he had been killed. This is the Christian belief.

Now, two thousand years later, there are millions of people all over the world who believe that Jesus is still alive today. His body can no longer be seen, but his spirit is everywhere. People can know him and talk to him in their prayers. They try to follow the example of his life on earth.

1.   (a) Where did Jesus live? (b) To which race of people did he belong?
2.   Copy the map, using coloured crayons or pens.
3.   (a) What does 'to be anointed' mean? (b) What do the words 'Messiah' and 'Christ' mean?
4.   Who is Jesus, according to Christian belief?
5.   What would Jesus probably have looked like?
6.   Write two or three sentences about the sort of life Jesus lived.
7.   What is happening in the photograph taken in Mexico?
8.   Look at the picture of the boat. What do the words on the banner mean?
9.   Describe the picture taken in Nazareth. The scene has probably changed little since Jesus's time. Note some of the things that would be different, e.g. what the old man is looking at.

2 The Bible

You would find a Bible in every church you went into today. Usually a large copy rests on a stand called a 'lectern'. A passage is read from it at church services. Here the Bible is being read by a priest at a Greek Orthodox service (see p.8).

The Bible is the Christians' holy book. It is about God. It tells what God is like and how people can come to know Him better.

Over many hundreds of years a number of holy men wrote about their history and their lives. They wrote poems and songs in praise of God. They told stories which helped to explain the truth about God. They set down rules saying how people should live their lives. These writings were collected together between 900 B.C. and A.D. 100 (see word list). Christians believe that these men were inspired by God and that what they wrote came from God. They believe that God speaks to people through the Bible, so it is called 'the Word of God'.

The Bible is divided into two parts. Christians call the first part the **Old Testament**. It contains thirty-nine 'books' about the history of the Jewish people and what they believed about God in the centuries before Jesus was born. It tells how they were expecting a 'Messiah', who would make a new beginning and bring joy and peace to the world. The second part is the **New Testament**. It tells the story of Jesus. He came to teach people about God, but not many recognized him as the expected Messiah. Four men called Matthew, Mark, Luke and John wrote in their Gospels what they knew and believed about Jesus Christ. The New Testament also tells of what happened to Jesus's followers in the thirty years after his death. It contains twenty-one of the letters they wrote to each other about how to live a true Christian life.

The writings of the Old Testament also form part of the Jewish holy scriptures. Jesus would have studied them as a boy. So Christians and Jews share many of the same beliefs about God. Muslims also think of many of the men in the Bible as men of God.

Look at question 5 opposite.

HOJNA   SIGENSE

PSMALS   EULK

                MUESAL

NRSOMA

                    PTREE

TTMWEAH

                LDEINA

XDEOSU

Every Christian has his own copy of the Bible. He may read it alone or with his family at home. Sometimes he will study the Bible with a group of other Christians, as this photograph shows.

The Bible is the world's best selling book. It has been translated into nearly every language. The first Bibles in England were written in Latin, like the one below. Latin was the language of the Romans, who brought Christianity to Britain, in about A.D. 200. In 1526 the New Testament was printed in English for the first time. In recent times the Bible has been rewritten in more modern words to make it easier to understand, but the stories and the meanings are the same in every copy.

The picture above shows some caves near the Dead Sea in Israel. In 1947 local shepherds discovered some very old manuscripts in one of the caves. These are now famous and are known as the 'Dead Sea Scrolls'. They are over two thousand years old: some of the earliest writings about the Old Testament ever found.

1. (a) What does B.C. mean? (b) What does A.D. mean?
2. Why do Christians call the Bible 'the Word of God'?
3. What are the two main parts of the Bible called?
4. What holy scriptures would Jesus have studied when he was a boy?
5. On p.4 the names of ten books in the Bible have been jumbled up. Can you sort them out?
6. (a) In the picture at the top of this page what are the people doing?
   (b) Is there anyone of about your age in the picture?
7. Write down the names of as many different versions of the Bible as you can find.
8. What are the 'Dead Sea Scrolls'?
9. Can you work out what the large Latin print says in the picture above?

3 What Jesus said

'Love God and love your neighbour as much as you love yourself.' This was part of the Jewish law. Jesus said that nothing was more important than to keep these commands. The evening before he died he acted out part of what he meant. Just before supper he knelt down and washed his disciples' feet. They were astonished, but he said, 'I, your Lord and Teacher, have just washed your feet. You then should wash one another's feet ... no slave is greater than his master and no messenger is greater than the one who sent him.' This day is now remembered as Maundy Thursday. In some churches there is a special service when the priest washes the feet of twelve men, as you can see below.

Jesus warned people, especially the priests, not to pretend to be very good and religious. He said, 'When you pray, or when you give something to a needy person, do not make a big show of it. God knows exactly how you are.'

THE SERMON ON THE MOUNT

The photograph above shows the Sea of Galilee. It was on a hill by this lake that Jesus gave a famous sermon (talk).

One day Jesus was out walking on these hills. Crowds of people followed him. They had seen him healing many people just by touching them. They wanted to know more about him, so they followed him. He sat down on the grass and the people sat around him. What he said to them was new. He wasn't telling them that their religion was wrong (remember they were Jews), he was adding to it. He was adding himself to it. He was making it come true. He reminded them about their laws: the Ten Commandments given by God to their great leader Moses, long ago. (Exodus,

Chapter 20.) Jesus said, 'One of those commandments was "You shall not murder", but I say that even if you hate someone, it is like murdering them in your heart.' In many churches the Ten Commandments are displayed on the wall.

Here, in modern words, are some of the other things he said that day: 'You must love your enemies as well as your friends. Don't be too concerned about money and possessions, trust God to take care of you. Do not criticize people, your own faults are probably worse. If you ask for the right things they will be given to you. If you search for answers in the right way you will learn them. Be humble, make peace, be merciful and pure in heart. Try to do good and have the courage to suffer for your belief in God. People who do this will belong to the Kingdom of God.'

Jesus taught them to pray to God with this prayer, known as the Lord's Prayer, which all Christians know by heart:

Our Father in heaven, hallowed be your name, your kingdom come, your will be done on earth as in heaven. Give us today our daily bread.
Forgive us our sins as we forgive those who sin against us.
Lead us not into temptation but deliver us from evil.

PARABLES

Often Jesus told stories to help people understand more about God. Notice the word 'Kingdom' in the sermon and the prayer above. Jesus taught that people should turn away from sin and follow his example if they wanted to belong to the 'Kingdom of God'. Many of his stories began: 'The Kingdom of God is like ...' (see Mark, Chapter 4). These and his other stories are called parables. In the Bible there are thirty-nine parables told by Jesus. They were usually about farmers and fishermen and family life, and other things his listeners would know about. But there is always a hidden meaning in them, about pride or greed or forgiveness, for example. The cartoon illustrates Matthew Chapter 18, verses 21-35.

Jesus told them this parable.

The King forgave him and let him go. But . . .

When the King heard, he was very angry and sent for the first man . . .

Jesus said, 'That is how God will treat each of you if you do not forgive your brother from your heart.'

1. What did Jesus say were the Jews' greatest commands?
2. Why is the priest washing someone's feet, in the photograph on p.6?
3. Describe what is happening in the drawing on p.6.
4. Write down three things Jesus said, in the Sermon on the Mount, that people should do.
5. Of all the sayings of Jesus on these pages which do you think would be hardest to obey?
6. What do you think the nun is doing in the photograph on p.6?
7. What is a 'parable'?
8. Look carefully at the cartoon strip. Write a modern parable of your own about forgiveness.

4 Christians

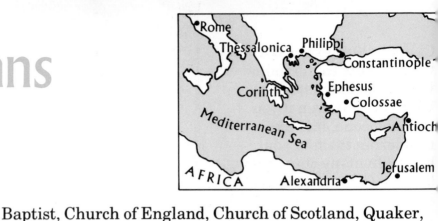

The Pope, leader of the Roman Catholic Church.

The Patriarch, leader of the Orthodox Church.

The Archbishop of Canterbury, head of the Anglican Church.

Baptist, Church of England, Church of Scotland, Quaker, Methodist, Orthodox, Pentecostal, Roman Catholic and United Reformed Church members are all Christians. How can this be? All these Christians share the same Bible. They all agree that Jesus Christ was God on earth, but they have disagreed about the way in which they should follow the example and teaching of Jesus. So different branches of Christianity have grown up, with different forms of worship.

The very first Christian groups met in Jerusalem. They spread Christianity to many other cities (shown on the map above). Over the years different Christian customs developed in different countries. Christian leaders, called bishops, would meet together from time to time to discuss and decide on matters of faith. However, the Bishops of Constantinople and Rome each struggled to be the most powerful. This, and other disagreements, led to a split in the Christian Church in 1054. The Eastern Orthodox Christians had their centre in Constantinople. The Roman Catholic Christians were led by the Bishop of Rome, who became known as the Pope (which means 'father').

Today most Orthodox Christians live in Greece, the U.S.S.R., Cyprus, Yugoslavia and America. You will also find Orthodox Christians in Britain. The word 'orthodox' means 'right belief'.

The Roman Catholic Church still has its headquarters in the Vatican in Rome. Its leader is still called the Pope. Today more than half the Christians in the world belong to the Roman Catholic Church. Catholic means 'world-wide'.

In 1520 a German priest called Martin Luther protested that the Church, with all its power and riches, its rules and its priests, often got in the way of ordinary people coming close to God. The Pope was very angry and had Luther expelled from the Church. But he and his followers went on protesting and their ideas spread to many other countries. The Churches that were set up became known as 'Protestant' Churches. The Church of England (or the Anglican Church) is a Protestant Church. Today there are Anglican Christians all over the world.

Other Churches listed at the beginning of the chapter are known as the 'Free Churches' because they are free from any government control. They have all started in the last 500 years. They do not have bishops. Both men and women can be ministers. Their churches are usually quite plain and their worship is simple and centred on Bible teaching. Here is a service in a United Reformed Church.

Jesus preached peace and love. But there have been times when Christians have gone to war 'in the name of Christ'. They have even tried to force other Christians to change their beliefs. Here you can see one Christian being tortured by others in 1581. Often a man would rather die than change his beliefs. So there has often been bad feeling between the Churches.

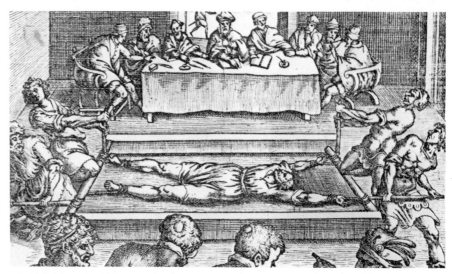

At last, during this century, the different Christian Churches are trying to work together. In some places they now share the same church building. These photographs show an open-air festival for all Christians, whatever their church or their race. A group of Chinese students are teaching Christian songs.

1. What are the two things that *all* Christians share?
2. How did the Protestants get their name?
3. Write down the title of the leader of: (a) the Orthodox Church; (b) the Roman Catholic Church; (c) the Church of England.
4. Look at the picture of the United Reformed church at the top of this page, the Anglican church on the cover and the Methodist church on p.18. What differences can you see?
5. Describe what is happening in the drawing on this page.
6. (a) What is written on the banner in the photograph above? (b) Why do you think it says that?
7. Look at the names of the books in the New Testament. You should be able to match six of them with the cities on the map on page 8, e.g. Ephesus and The Letter to the Ephesians.

5 What Christians believe

On these two pages all the words in green make up the Christian creed. The word 'creed' comes from the Latin word 'credo', meaning 'I believe'. It has been used by Christians since the early years of the Church. Most Christians learn their creed by heart and it is often recited at church services. A creed sets down some of the most important things that a Christian should believe and try to understand about his religion. It says what he shares with other Christians all over the world and it explains the Christian belief to non-Christians.

I believe in God the Father Almighty, maker of heaven and earth.

Christians, like Jews, Muslims and Sikhs, believe there is only one God. He is all powerful and he is good. He created the world.

And in Jesus Christ, his only Son our Lord, who was conceived by the power of the Holy Spirit and born of the Virgin Mary.

Jesus is God's son. He was born from a human mother whose name was Mary. The Bible says Mary was still a virgin when she became pregnant ('virgin' means she had not made love with a man). Mary was already expecting her baby when she married Joseph. God the Holy Spirit made Jesus special from the beginning. He was human and he was God. Mary is especially important to Roman Catholics.

He suffered under Pontius Pilate, was crucified, died and was buried. He descended to the dead.

Pontius Pilate was the Roman governor in Jerusalem. He judged Jesus and ordered that he should be crucified. Jesus died on the cross and his body was carried away and buried in a tomb carved out of rock. A stone was rolled across the entrance and the tomb was guarded by Roman soldiers. Jesus joined those who had already died.

On the third day he rose again from the dead.

Two days later the tomb was found empty. Jesus appeared alive to his disciples. They talked and ate with him *after* he had died on the cross. God had given him new life.

He ascended into heaven and is seated at the right hand of the Father.

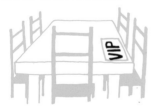

'Ascended' means 'went up'. People used to believe that the earth was flat and heaven was up above it. Christians today do not believe that Jesus is 'up in the sky'. They believe that his body has gone away: he cannot be seen, he is part of God. God is everywhere. He is in the world, and in the hearts and minds of human beings. The place of honour is always on the right-hand side of the host. Jesus has the place of honour with God.

He will come
again to judge
the living
and the dead.

All people are judged by God. When they die they will either be taken to be with God (heaven) or they will be cut off from God (hell). This depends on two things: (1) what they have believed about God and Jesus; (2) how they have lived their lives on earth.

I believe in the Holy Spirit.

Religious people believe that God is spirit, because anything with a body has limits and God has no limits. Christians say the Holy Spirit gives them faith; it helps them to pray, to be wise and kind and it brings them joy and peace.

I believe in the holy catholic Church and the communion of saints.

The buildings in which Christians worship are called churches. But the Church also means all the *people* who follow Jesus. (Here, catholic means world-wide, not Roman Catholic.) Communion means fellowship, a sharing of the spirit. A Christian needs to meet and share with other Christians. There is more about saints on p.25.

I believe in the forgiveness of sins.

To sin means to do something wrong. Jesus said that if a person does wrong to another person, he does wrong to God. No one is perfectly good; everyone sins. But if you are truly sorry God will forgive you. You can stop feeling guilty and make a new start. You must also forgive anyone who does wrong to you.

I believe in the resurrection of the body and the life everlasting.

Resurrection means 'rising up'. Jesus rose from death to new life: new because he could come and go suddenly, sometimes through locked doors. His friends recognized him and spoke to him several times before he went from their sight for the last time. Jesus continues to live. Christians believe that they will also rise to new life although it is impossible to understand exactly how this will be.

1. Write down one reason for having a creed.
2. Which other religions believe in only one God?
3. What happened when someone was crucified? (See also the word list and the picture on p.3.)
4. What are the two men doing in the drawing on p.10? (John, Chapter 19, verses 38–42 will help you.)
5. (a) Where is Jesus now, according to Christian belief? (b) Where is God?
6. A pair of scales is a symbol of judgement. What do Christians believe will happen to them when they die?
7. A dove is a symbol of peace. Why do you think it is used as a symbol for the Holy Spirit?
8. What does 'communion' mean?
9. Copy and complete this sentence: Christians say that Jesus rose from ... to ... .
10. Copy the last drawing on this page and write a caption for it. (John, Chapter 20, verses 19–29 will help you.)

6 What Christians do

These two pages show some of the ways in which Christians try to obey Jesus's command: 'Love God and love your neighbour as much as you love yourself'.

THEY TEACH

Christians teach their children about Jesus. 'Sunday school' or 'Junior Church' is usually held each week to teach children about their religion.

THEY PRAY AND STUDY

A Christian prays to God each day. He may pray with others or alone. Often he kneels and closes his eyes. There is more about Bible study in Chapter 3.

THEY GO TO CHURCH

This photograph was taken in Zaire after morning service. A Christian goes to his local church most Sundays, along with other Christians, to worship God.

THEY HELP THE NEEDY

These men would have died on the streets of Calcutta in India if Mother Teresa and her nurses had not saved them. Mother Teresa is a nursing nun from Yugoslavia. She spends her life looking after sick and dying people. All Christians should help those in need.

THEY GIVE MONEY

A Christian should give a certain amount of money each week to the church. Some of this is for the upkeep of the church building and the general running of the church. Some will go to people in need. Money is usually collected at church services.

THEY WORK FOR PEACE

These people are marching to a meeting of prayer for peace. All Christians pray and work for peace and justice. Quakers (the Society of Friends) are 'pacifists': they believe that if you follow the teaching and life of Jesus, you cannot take part in war or violence.

Some Christians become ministers in the Church
(see Chapter 10). Some become missionaries (see p.14).
Some Christians join communities of monks, who usually
live in a monastery. A monk is a man who decides to give
his whole life to God. He makes three promises: 1. To live
a simple life with no money or possessions of his own.
2. Not to marry. 3. To obey God and the monk in charge.
He spends much of his time praying. The work of running
the monastery, such as cooking, is shared by all the monks.
The members of some orders are called friars; they often go
out to work among people in need. A woman who gives her
life to God is called a nun. She usually lives in a convent.
The plain robes worn by most monks and nuns are called
habits. (There are more photographs on pp.6, 19 and 25.)

Some people work for Christian organizations. They may
make it their full-time paid job or they may work part
time for nothing. Here are three such organizations.

THE CHURCH ARMY

The Church Army was
started about a hundred
years ago to help poor people
and to tell them about
Jesus. Above you can see a
Church Army officer
reading aloud to an old
lady. She lives in one of the
Church Army homes for old
people. They also run homes
for homeless people and for
young people in trouble.

CHRISTIAN AID

Christian Aid gave money
to these African farmers
to buy ploughs. Money is
collected from people who
have enough and sent to
people who do not have
enough. 'The Good
Samaritan' is a story told
by Jesus to show that your
'neighbour' is any person in
the world who needs your
help (Luke, Chapter 10).

SIMON COMMUNITY

It is very early morning.
This 'Simon' van is full of
hot soup and sandwiches for
these men who have spent
the night sleeping out on
the streets. Simon
Community workers try to
help those whom no one else
cares about. They get their
name from Simon of Cyrene,
who helped Jesus carry his
cross (Mark, Chapter 15).

1. Write down four things that every Christian does.
2. What is 'Sunday school' or 'Junior Church'?
3. What are the people doing in the photograph taken in Zaire?
4. Who is Mother Teresa?
5. What use is made of the money that Christians give?
6. Look at the picture of people marching. Why are they doing this?
7. (a) What three promises do monks and nuns make? (b) What is happening to the monk in the picture?
8. Draw one of the pictures in this chapter and write a sentence about it.
9. Imagine that you work for one of the three Christian organizations described above. Write a short story
   describing a day's work.

7 Spreading the gospel

The Gospels of Matthew, Mark, Luke and John are the first books in the New Testament. They are about Jesus. The word 'gospel' means 'good news'.

The very last thing Jesus said to his disciples was: 'Go and preach the gospel to people all over the world.' They were to tell people that if they believed in Jesus and followed his example and teaching their sins would be forgiven and they would belong to the Kingdom of God (see p.7). Every Christian should tell others about Jesus. Those who travel about the world to spread the gospel are called 'missionaries'.

St Paul was the first great missionary. He worked with Jesus's disciples to start Churches in many cities (shown on the map on p.8). You can read about his adventures in the Bible in the book of Acts.

Some Christians today use badges or stickers to show what they believe.

Above is the Church Missionary Society building in London. Three missionaries from Uganda have come to Britain. Christian missionaries today are sent by their Church to work with Christians in other countries. They may go for two or three years or they may spend their whole lives teaching about Jesus far from home. Often missionaries are doctors or nurses, teachers or ministers. The very first hospitals and schools in many countries have been started by Christian missionaries. The picture below shows a missionary in Pakistan teaching mentally handicapped boys how to weave.

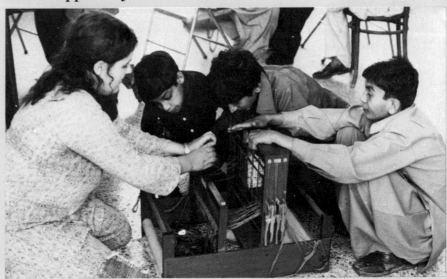

One way of spreading the gospel is through books. SPCK stands for the Society for the Promotion (spreading) of Christian Knowledge. There are SPCK bookshops all over the world. The Bible has been translated into nearly every language.

Billy Graham is a well-known American preacher of the gospel. Huge crowds go to hear him speak. However, even today there are some parts of the world where Christians have to meet in secret. There are countries where Christians may be unable to obtain jobs. In the U.S.S.R., for example, it is against the law to teach religion to groups of children under the age of eighteen.

The map below shows the places where Christianity is the main religion in the world today.

The Salvation Army is often to be seen out on the streets and in parks, spreading the gospel through music and singing. It also helps many thousands of people in need through its homes, hostels and workshops.

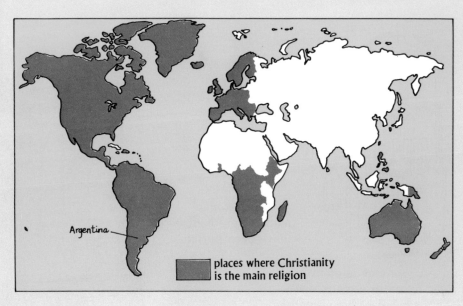

Argentina

places where Christianity is the main religion

8 Churches

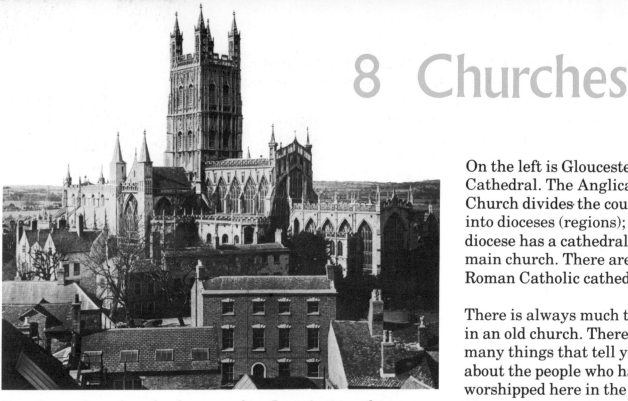

For about three hundred years after Jesus's time there were no church buildings. Christians used to meet in one another's homes. (See p.28.) However, when the persecution by the Romans ended, Christians began to construct large buildings where many of them could meet together to worship God. Since then thousands of churches of all sizes and shapes have been built all over the world.

On the left is Gloucester Cathedral. The Anglican Church divides the country into dioceses (regions); each diocese has a cathedral as its main church. There are also Roman Catholic cathedrals.

There is always much to see in an old church. There are many things that tell you about the people who have worshipped here in the past. If you want to find out more about your ancestors you might look at the gravestones and in the books which contain details of all the baptisms, weddings and funerals that have happened in that church.

Bell tower.
Bells are rung to tell people when a service is about to take place, and also at weddings. This is how they work.

wheels

bells

ropes

Gravestones mark where bodies have been buried.

A yew tree is often to be found in a churchyard. It is a symbol of life going on for ever, both because it is evergreen and because it lives for a very long time.

Churchyard.
The land inside the wall is holy ground. It has been blessed by a bishop (see p.20).

Sunday is the day of the week set aside by most Christians for worship. A Christian tries to go to a service in his local church every Sunday. Most churches also have services on weekdays. You can read more about church services in Chapters 9, 11, 12 and 13. Churches used to be always open so that anyone could go in to look round or to pray. However, some churches are now locked for security reasons and you have to borrow the key to go in.

Many modern churches are known as church centres. This means that part of the building is a church, but there are also other rooms used for such events as Bible study groups, Sunday school, youth clubs, playgroups, parties, jumble sales, Boys' Brigade, Girl Guides, Scouts, clubs for old people. In other words it is a place where people in the area can meet for friendship, help, fun and advice.

This page shows the inside of a modern Anglican church.

The **piano** on which music is played. (In many churches an **organ** is used.)

This door leads into the **vestry**. This is the small room where the robes are kept for clergy (and the **choir,** who lead the singing).

You will find the symbol of a **cross** in many parts of a church building.

The **font** where people are baptized. It holds water. (See Chapter 13.)

The **lectern** from which the Bible is read.

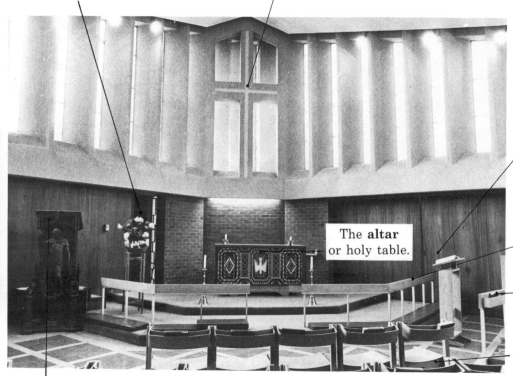

These doors lead into a big hall and other smaller meeting-rooms.

The **altar rail.** People kneel here to take the bread and wine at a Communion service.

The **altar** or holy table.

Books containing **hymns** (songs) and **prayers.**

The **pews** or chairs where people sit. They may kneel on cushions or **hassocks** when they pray.

The **pulpit** from which the priest preaches the word of God to the people.

1. (a) What is a cathedral? (b) Do you know the name of the cathedral nearest to you?
2. Where would you look in a church to find out more about your ancestors?
3. Why should you treat a churchyard with respect?
4. Make a drawing to show how church bells work.
5. Write down a few things a church centre might be used for.
6. Give the meaning of these words: (a) vestry, (b) choir, (c) pews, (d) hassock, (e) altar, (f) lectern, (g) hymn, (h) pulpit, (i) font.
7. If you go to a church or any other place of worship write a few sentences describing the building. If not, find your own picture of the inside of a church and describe it. (The cover of this book might help you.)

9 Worship

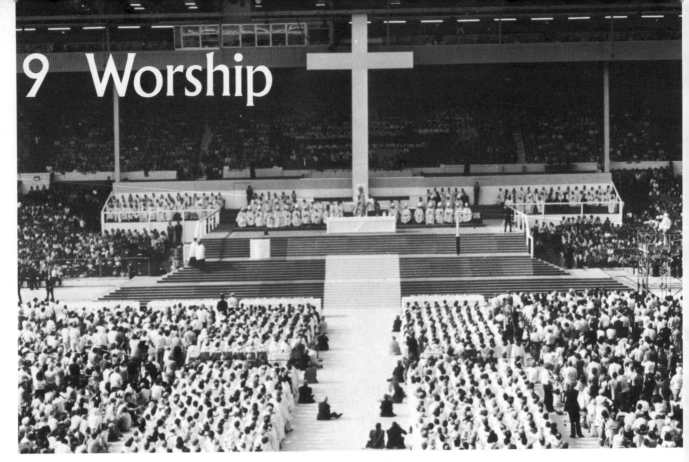

To worship means to honour, adore and praise someone far greater than yourself. Christians use different ways of worshipping God. They want to thank, praise, obey and love God, and to ask for His forgiveness.

Singing and music is important in much Christian worship. This Anglican choir spends several hours each week practising for the services.

The thousands of Christians in the picture above have come to worship God at a service led by the Pope at Wembley stadium.

Below is a picture of morning worship at a Methodist church. The congregation (gathering of worshippers) pray together and sing hymns together. Can you see the hymn numbers on the board? The minister is standing in the pulpit. After a passage from the Bible has been read, he will preach a sermon. The sermon will help to explain the Bible passage and teach about Christian living today. For Roman Catholics and most Anglicans the Mass (or Holy Communion or Eucharist) is the most important Sunday service (see p.22). There are different services for weddings, baptisms, funerals and other special occasions. Services are usually led by the minister.

Pentecostal Christians, like these in Argentina, often sing, dance, clap and raise their hands in worship.

Worship is very quiet for these nuns in their convent. They have eight short services every day.

Confession is the 'being sorry' part of worship. Roman Catholics confess to their priests. These people in Poland will go, one by one, to sit or kneel in the 'cubicle'. They will confess (own up to) the things they have done wrong. The priest can forgive them in God's name and advise them how to be better in future.

Above are two women worshipping. The crippled woman on the left has made a pilgrimage to Lourdes in France. It is said that in 1858 a young woman called Bernadette saw a vision of the Virgin Mary. (A vision is something seen in a kind of dream.) The water from a spring at Lourdes is believed to be holy. Thousands of sick people go there each year and there have been many miracles of healing.

The other woman, who is Greek Orthodox, worships God in the quiet of her own bedroom. She has a collection of holy objects which help her to concentrate on God.

On pp.28–30 you can find out about some of the symbols which help Christians to worship.

1. Look at the photograph taken at Wembley. How can you tell it is a Christian service?
2. What do Christians want to do when they worship God?
3. What does a choir do?
4. What is a sermon?
5. In what way is the nuns' worship different from Pentecostal worship?
6. In the photograph taken in Poland, what are the people doing?
7. Why is Lourdes famous?
8. What can you see in the photograph of the Greek Orthodox woman?
9. Draw or describe four things that happen at a church service.

10 Ministers

Other names for the leader of a church are priest, rector, vicar, pastor, elder, chaplain, clergyman and Father. The Roman Catholic Church allows only men to be priests. They must not marry; they expect to give their whole life to their church work. The Church of England also has only men priests, but women may become deacons and help with the priests' work. The Free Churches have both men and women ministers. A bishop is a senior church leader. He has charge of a region (called a diocese) with its churches and ministers. In Britain there are about one hundred Anglican bishops and about fifty Roman Catholic bishops. The Free Churches do not have bishops.

an Anglican vicar
dog collar
surplice
stole
cassock

a Roman Catholic priest
chasuble
girdle
stole
alb

preaching band
cassock
preaching gown

a Free Church minister

bishop's crook
mitre
cope

a bishop

You can recognize a minister by the 'dog-collar' he often wears. Special clothes are usually worn in church. They may be modern and simple or old and decorative.

The men on the left are at a Roman Catholic college where they are learning to become priests. They study the Bible, learn how to conduct services and preach sermons and how to look after people's special needs. When they have finished their training and passed the exams they will be ordained. Ordination is a very special service when the bishop lays his hands on each man's head and blesses him for his future ministry. On the right you can see a man being ordained.

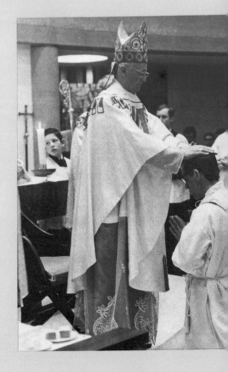

WHAT DOES A MINISTER DO?

Here is a page from a city minister's diary:

SUN	8am Communion service (call in on Sunday school (10.15)) 5pm healing service 11am service 3pm Youth group
MON	9.10 School assembly Letters (Mrs M. here to type) 7pm School managers meeting 2pm meeting in Town Hall (unemployment) 9pm meet Bob (curate) at the pub!
TUES	10.30 funeral ~~11.30~~ 11.45 funeral 7.30 Confirmation class Visit: Bonfields " Mrs O. (sick) 9.30 visit Mr Denny (about money for roof) " Marie (Sunday School)
WED	10.am Communion service 11am service at Earlsbury Grange (Old People's Home) 7.30 Baptism preparation 4pm See Mr P. (church warden) (film strip)
THUR	DAY OFF
FRI	visit Mrs C. in hospital (ward 16) *NB write report on church hall* 8pm prayer group at vicarage Ken (organist) here 11.30 12.30 lunch club (for old folk)
SAT	church leaflet 3pm wedding JUMBLE SALE in hall 11am 4pm Youth club leaders' meeting write sermon

A chaplain is a minister who does not have a parish. He may be chaplain to a prison, a ship, a university, a hospital or a factory or to the army, navy or air force. Below is a hospital chaplain blessing a new-born baby.

In the picture below a chaplain is visiting some factory workers.

These are all the events that were fixed in advance. As well as these things the doorbell and the telephone often ring: people want the minister's help or advice with a problem. Most ministers have charge of a church and a parish. (The parish is the district around the church and the people who live there.) In the country each minister may look after more than one church. Sometimes a minister has an assistant (a deacon or a curate) to help him.

1. What does a bishop do?
2. When students are training to become ministers what do they learn?
3. What happens at an ordination service?
4. Look at the diary. What was the minister doing on: (a) Wednesday evening? (b) Friday evening?
5. How many meetings did the minister go to that week? What were they about?
6. Choose one of the two photographs above and describe what the chaplain is doing.
7. Copy one or two of the drawings on the opposite page. Label and colour them. Why do you think ministers wear clothes that are different from other people's?

21

11 Easter time

Easter is the most important festival of the year for Christians. It takes place some time between 22 March and 25 April, according to the moon. Christians remember the death of Jesus and celebrate his resurrection; this is the word they use for 'coming to life again' (see Chapter 5).

Easter eggs have nothing to do with the Bible, but an egg contains a new life and so it has become a symbol for the resurrection – the new life of Jesus. These eggs are from Hungary, where it is the custom to paint eggs with colourful patterns for Easter.

LENT

The forty days before Easter are known as Lent. This is the time when Christians prepare themselves for Easter. They study the Bible. Many fast (go without food for a certain time) or give up something they like doing. This is to remind them of the forty days when Jesus was tempted by the Devil in the desert, before he began his teaching (see Matthew, Chapter 4).

PALM SUNDAY

The week before Easter is called Holy Week. It starts with Palm Sunday. At the church service everyone is given a palm leaf made into the shape of a cross. On the Sunday before he died, Jesus rode into Jerusalem on a donkey. It was the time of the Jewish Passover, when Jerusalem was full of people. As Jesus passed crowds of people cheered and waved palm branches and shouted: 'Hosanna! God bless the king who comes in the name of the Lord.' (Read Matthew, Chapter 21.) Many Christians try to make a pilgrimage at Easter time to the holy places in Israel where Jesus lived. In this picture pilgrims from France are carrying palm branches along the way that Jesus rode into Jerusalem.

MAUNDY THURSDAY

Thursday was the night when Jesus and his disciples had their last meal together. Before supper Jesus washed his disciples' feet and commanded them to serve one another (see p.6). 'Mandatum' means 'command', which is how Maundy Thursday got its name. During the meal Jesus blessed the bread and, as he broke some off, he said, 'My body will be broken like this; remember me when you break bread.' Then he drank from the cup of wine and passed it round, saying, 'My blood will be spilt; remember me when you drink wine.' Christians are doing what Jesus asked them when they have bread (his body) and wine (his blood) at their service of Holy Communion. At this moment they feel that Jesus is really present with them.

Jesus's enemies had been plotting against him. The Jewish religious leaders did not believe he was God's son and they were worried because he was so popular. They plotted to have him arrested and they made up charges against him. Jesus went on trial before the Roman governor, Pontius Pilate, who was afraid that Jesus might be stirring up a rebellion against Roman rule.

GOOD FRIDAY

The Gospels tell how Jesus was tried, mocked, beaten and at last crucified on the Friday. It is called 'Good Friday' now; Christians think of it as the day when good won over evil. They say that because Jesus died he made it possible for people to understand just how much God loves them.

In this picture the story of Jesus's crucifixion is being acted out in Mexico. Jesus carries the heavy wooden cross on which he will die.

EASTER DAY

On the Sunday when some of Jesus's followers went to the tomb where he had been buried, they found it empty. Before he died, Jesus had told the disciples that he would return to life again, but still they did not understand what had happened. Later, when Jesus appeared to them, they believed he had risen and in some mysterious way was alive and with them.

Christians ever since then have shared that belief. If you go into a church on Easter Day you may hear Christians greet each other by saying, 'Christ is risen' and the answer will be 'He is risen indeed'. The church will be filled with flowers and there will be much joy. Children built this 'tomb' in their church on Good Friday. On Easter Day they rolled away the stone and covered the tomb with flowers.

1. What do Christians do during Lent?
2. Why are Easter eggs given at Easter? (Besides the fact that they taste good!)
3. (a) Why is Palm Sunday so called? (b) What happens at a service on Palm Sunday?
4. If you look at one of the photographs on p.6 you will see how Maundy Thursday got its name. Write out the command that Jesus gave.
5. What is the old man doing in the photograph opposite?
6. Why did some people plot against Jesus?
7. Describe what is happening in the photograph taken in Mexico.
8. According to Christians, what happened on the first Easter Day?
9. Design an Easter card or paint a hard-boiled egg with Easter symbols. (Chapter 14 may help you.)

12 Other festivals

CHRISTMAS

Christmas is Christ's birthday. Every year on 25 December Christians remember the birth of Jesus Christ. Most countries count their years from the birth of Christ (see p.1). In many churches and Christian homes at Christmas time you will find a 'nativity' model. Usually there will be a baby in a crib, his parents, some shepherds, a donkey, an ox, some angels and a big star. This was the scene when Jesus was born. Sometimes, in a church or a school, a group of children act the story of Jesus's birth. It is told in Matthew, Chapters 1 and 2 and Luke, Chapter 2.

Groups of Christians go around the streets singing carols at Christmas time. The singers below are from Norway. Christmas carols are songs about Jesus's birth. Many churches hold a special carol service at which the stories about Jesus's birth are read aloud from the Bible.

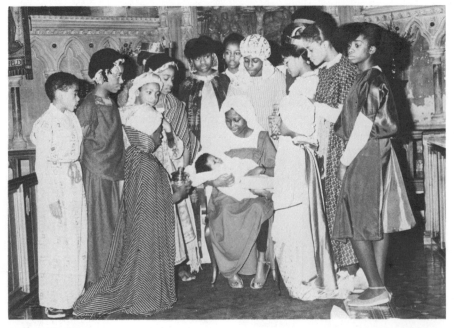

ADVENT

The four weeks before Christmas are called Advent, which means 'coming'. It is a time of solemn preparation for the coming of Jesus into the world. An Advent wreath has four candles which are lit, one by one, on each of the four Sundays before Christmas. These remind Christians of Jesus as 'the Light of the World' (see John, Chapter 8, verse 12).

Have you seen an Advent calendar like this one on the right? It has twenty-four little windows to be opened by children, day by day, for the twenty-four days before Christmas.

Above The Prophet's Mosque in Medina. Muhammad's tomb lies beneath the green dome.

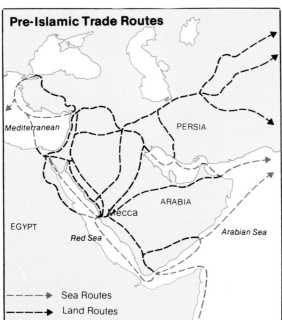

Pre-Islamic Trade Routes

Mediterranean

PERSIA

EGYPT

Mecca

Red Sea

ARABIA

Arabian Sea

- - - → Sea Routes
▬ ▬ → Land Routes

Right Mecca during the lifetime of the Prophet was connected to many other countries by sea and land trade-routes.

The return to Mecca

While they were at Medina, raids and battles took place between the Muslims and the people of Mecca. At last, in 630 the Meccans were defeated and Muhammad returned in triumph to Mecca. The people accepted Islam as their religion and the idols were taken from the Ka'aba and destroyed.

In 632 Muhammad died. Abu Bakr, his close friend, told the people 'If there are any among you who worshipped Muhammad, he is dead. But if it is God you worship, He lives forever.'

'The prophets leave knowledge as their inheritance. The learned ones inherit this great fortune.'

saying of the Prophet Muhammad

How Islam spread

Right A century after the death of Muhammad the Muslims ruled an area stretching from the borders of India to Spain. Apart from Spain, the areas shown in green are still Muslim today.

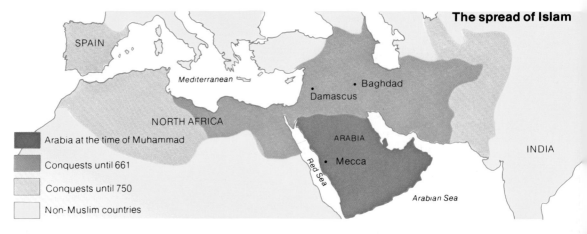

The spread of Islam

- Arabia at the time of Muhammad
- Conquests until 661
- Conquests until 750
- Non-Muslim countries

Muslim rule expands

After Muhammad's death some of the tribes who had become Muslims decided to give up Islam because they did not want to pay *zakat*. The Muslims chose Abu Bakr to be Caliph (*Khalifa* means successor).

He went to war against the tribes who had deserted Islam until they submitted. After the Muslims had conquered all Arabia they turned against the non-Muslim empires of Byzantium and Persia. Within a century a vast area was under Muslim rule.

Right The Court of the Myrtles, at the Palace of the Alhambra, at Granada in southern Spain. The Spanish language and Spanish architecture still bear many traces of the seven centuries of Moorish rule.

The Muslims allowed the Christians and Jews in these lands to keep their religions but made them pay extra taxes.

Shiites and Sunni

Abu Bakr was followed as Caliph by other close companions of the Prophet—Umar and Uthman. In 656 Ali (Muhammad's cousin and son-in-law) became Caliph but he was murdered in 661 and was succeeded by a member of the Umayyad family. Ali's supporters, the *Shi'at-Ali* (party of Ali) carried on fighting for his son Hussein, who was killed in 680.

The descendants of these people became known as the Shia or Shiites. They are a minority group in Islam and have some beliefs and customs which differ from the majority, called Sunni, who follow the *Sunna* (tradition) of the Prophet. Nowadays the Shia form the majority of the population in Iraq and Iran.

Baghdad—the new capital

The Umayyad dynasty was overthrown in 750 by descendants of the Prophet's uncle, Abbas. The Abbasids moved the capital of the empire from Damascus to the new city of Baghdad. When Baghdad was destroyed by the Mongols in 1258 the Abbasids' rule ended.

By then the empire had for some time ceased to be one territory ruled from a single centre. Local princes and generals tried to make themselves independent wherever they could. At one time there were three rulers claiming to be Caliph. But as a civilization Islam remained united by the Arabic language, by laws based on the Qur'an and by ties of trade and pilgrimage.

Below The Dome of the Rock in Jerusalem, third holiest city of Islam, is the first great Muslim building. Built at the end of the 7th century, it was restored in the 16th century by the Ottoman architect Sinan. Muslims believe that the rock sheltered by this mosque is the spot from which the call to judgement will be sounded on the last day.

Islamic empires

Right In the 16th and 17th centuries the Ottoman, Safavid and Mughal empires dazzled Europeans with their power and splendour.

The greatest extent of the major Islamic Empires

Vienna •

• Istanbul

Mediterranean Sea

Isfahan • PERSIA

EGYPT

ARABIA

AFRICA

• Delhi

Fatehpur Sikri • • Agra

INDIA

Indian Ocean

Ottoman

Safavid

Mughal

The Ottoman Empire

Of the three great Muslim empires which had been founded by the mid-16th century the Ottoman Empire was the one which lasted the longest. It began with the 13th-century conquests of Osman, a Turkish nomad chief. Osman's descendants crushed the Byzantine Empire and after 1453 made its capital (Constantinople) their own, but re-named it Istanbul. The court of Suleyman II so dazzled European visitors that they called him 'the Magnificent'.

Right The Shah's Mosque, Isfahan, is still the glory of this purpose-built capital.

The Ottomans twice laid siege to Vienna but the climate and great distances involved set limits on their powers of conquest. In 1699 the Ottomans signed a treaty giving up territory for the first time but it was only defeat in the First World War (1914–18) that finally brought the empire to an end.

The Safavid Empire

The Ottomans fought many border wars against the Safavid rulers of Persia, whose main achievement was to make Shiite Islam the official religion of their country. Under Shah Abbas a magnificent new capital was built at Isfahan. In the 18th century the Safavids were followed by the weak Qajar dynasty.

The Mughal Empire

Safavid Persia also fought against its other neighbour, the Mughal Empire. The Mughal Empire was founded by Babur, almost lost by his son Humayun but regained by Akbar (Babur's grandson) who doubled the size of its territory.

Akbar reigned at almost exactly the same time as Queen Elizabeth I of England. Like her he was a great patron of the arts and lavishly praised by courtiers. He built massive palace forts at Delhi and Agra as well as a whole new capital at Fatehpur Sikri which was abandoned almost as soon as it was completed.

In 1739 the Persians sacked Delhi and carried off a fabulous, jewelled Peacock throne. The Mughal Empire never really recovered and its power passed gradually into the hands of the British, who stayed as rulers until 1947.

Common features

These three Islamic empires—Ottoman, Safavid and Mughal—had a number of features in common. The ruling class was not Arab in those empires. The Ottomans relied on Christian converts, recruited as boys, to serve as civil servants and members of the famed Janissary corps of troops. In each empire the power of gunpowder was used to make remote provinces obey the power of central government. Each court was a place of splendour, luxury and intrigue. Each, at its height, was more powerful than any comparable state in Europe.

15

The Qur'an

The actual word of God

Muslims believe that the Qur'an is the actual word of God. Muhammad was not, therefore, the 'author' of the Qur'an. Muslims believe that Muhammad was the man through whom God chose to speak to mankind. The word *Qur'an* in Arabic means 'recitation'. The first lines revealed to the Prophet begin with the command 'Recite'.

During the lifetime of the Prophet various parts of the Qur'an were written down. A number of the early Muslims learned them by heart. After the Prophet's death a final version of the Qur'an was put together, and Muslims believe that this represents God's last and complete message to mankind.

The Qur'an is arranged in 114 suras (chapters), each of which has a name. These do not occur in the order in which they were revealed to the Prophet. Scholars generally regard Sura 96 (The Congealed Blood) as the one that was first revealed to Muhammad. The first sura *Al-Fatihah* (The Opening) is recited in each of the daily prayers. Apart from this one, the other suras are organized in the approximate order of their length, with the longer suras coming at the beginning and the shorter ones at the end. This roughly reverses the order in which they came to the Prophet. The shorter suras, revealed while he was still at Mecca, tell of God and Judgement and Heaven and Hell.

Rules for living

The longer suras, revealed when he was leading the Muslim community at Medina, contain more detailed rules about how Muslims should live.

Muslims believe that because the Qur'an is God's final revelation to mankind it is perfect. They believe that the holy books of the Christians and the Jews, the Gospels and the Torah, are to be respected but that they do not contain the truth of God's message intact.

Because Muslims believe that the Qur'an is God's actual and final word they regard it as the most important book in the world. Traditional education in Muslim countries has always been based on a most detailed study of the Qur'an. Many scholars learn it completely by heart.

No translation except for study

Muslims also believe that the Qur'an, which was revealed in Arabic, cannot be translated adequately. Any translation misses something of its meaning. Therefore Muslims always learn it in Arabic, though for many of them it is not the language they usually speak. Translations may be used for the purpose of study.

The Qur'an is composed in a style which is half-prose and half-poetry. It has a very strong rhythm which has a powerful effect on Muslims who hear it read aloud. When Muhammad began to proclaim his revelation many of the unbelievers in Mecca called on him to perform miracles to prove that he was a prophet. Muhammad replied that he was an ordinary man and not divine. His only miracle was the Qur'an itself. The people who heard it had to admit that it was language of the greatest power and beauty.

Muslims believe that this power and beauty is proof of the Qur'an's divine origin. Ever since Muhammad, the Qur'an has been regarded as the most perfect use of the Arabic language.

Because Muslims regard the Qur'an as God's word they treat copies of it with the greatest respect. It is usually kept wrapped up and placed on a shelf for safety. While it is being read aloud Muslims will sit quietly, listening with complete attention.

'The best of you is he who has learnt the Qur'an and then taught it.'

'None of you has faith unless I am dearer to him than his father, and his son and all mankind.'

sayings of the Prophet Muhammad

Right The Qur'an has always been the foundation of education throughout the Muslim world. Believers are encouraged to learn by heart as much of it as they can.

The Five Pillars

Belief and action

Ask any Muslim to explain Islam and it is quite likely that he or she will talk about the 'five pillars of the faith'. It is important to note that these are matters of action as well as belief. They involve the individual believer in acting with others as a member of a world-wide religious community.

The first pillar

The first pillar is the profession of faith (*shahadah*)—'*I witness that there is no god but Allah and that Muhammad is the Prophet of Allah.*' Anyone who makes this statement publicly and sincerely can become a Muslim by that simple act.

Muslims believe that Allah 'the Merciful, the Compassionate' made the world, is all-powerful and all-seeing. He will judge all men and women at the end of time, sending them to Hell or Heaven according to their deeds. Muslims revere Jesus as a Prophet among many other Prophets such as Moses and Abraham but do not believe that he was divine. This is the main difference of belief that separates them from Christians.

Right Muslims see in the fruitfulness and beauty of a garden clear proof of God as the Creator of the World.

Right Each of the five daily prayers consists of a set cycle of ritual movements and prayers in Arabic which denote the believers' willing submission to God.

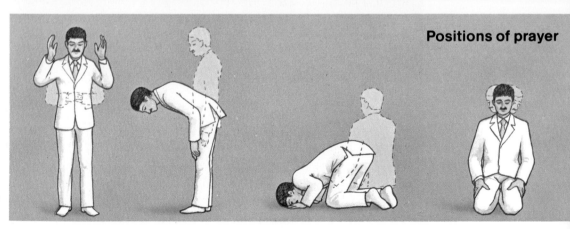

Positions of prayer

The second pillar

The second pillar is prayer five times a day (*salat*). Before praying a Muslim must wash his face, arms, head and feet. The prayers are said in Arabic and follow a fixed series of words and movements.

Prayers may be said in any clean place but adult male Muslims should go to the mosque for the noon prayer on Fridays. Prayer serves as a constant reminder of God's teachings to mankind and man's duty to praise and obey Him.

The third pillar

The third pillar of the faith is *zakat*, the act of giving each year a set proportion of one's wealth to help the needy and to support such good causes as building mosques or providing scholarships for students.

The fourth and fifth pillars

The fourth and fifth pillars are fasting in the month of Ramadan (*saum*) (see pp 22–23) and making the pilgrimage to Mecca (*hajj*) (see pp 24–25). Muslims are also obliged by their faith to be honest, just and generous and to be ready to fight in its defence. They are also forbidden to eat pork, to drink alcohol, to gamble or to lend money for interest.

Muslims believe that these rules are based on God's commands and cannot be altered. They provide a framework for a healthy society in which the religion, wealth and honour of all are made safe and secure.

'Worship Allah as if you see Him; if you do not see Him, know that He sees you.'

saying of the Prophet Muhammad

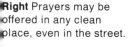

Right Prayers may be offered in any clean place, even in the street.

Mosques

Simple beginnings

The first mosque was built in Medina by the Prophet and his closest followers. It was a very simple building with a roof of palm fronds held up by tree trunks. Many mosques of the early conquest years were converted Christian churches. Others, like the great mosque at Kairouan, in Tunisia, were built from stones and pillars taken from Roman ruins. Gradually Muslim architects began to design splendid buildings such as the Dome of the Rock mosque in Jerusalem and the Ibn Tulun mosque in Cairo.

Similar basic design

Mosques vary greatly in detail. In West Africa they are normally built of mud, in Iran they are often surfaced with tiles, but most have the same general features. There is an open courtyard with a water supply, where worshippers can gather and wash before going into the covered area of the prayer-hall. This is often divided into two parts to separate men and women. There are no pews because Muslims need the floor to pray on.

Muslims always pray facing towards

Mecca so it is important for them to know the *qibla* (the direction of prayer). The qibla wall therefore contains an empty arch, the *mihrab*, which indicates the direction of Mecca. Next to the mihrab there is often a *minbar*, a pulpit with steps, from which the sermon is given at the noon prayer on Friday. Large mosques have an official *imam* (prayer leader) to give the sermon and lead the prayers but any adult male Muslim can lead the prayers if necessary.

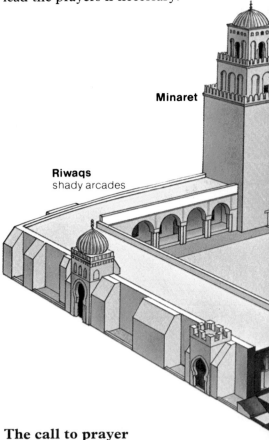

Minaret

Riwaqs
shady arcades

The call to prayer

The most noticeable external feature of the mosque is the minaret, a tall tower from which the muezzin calls the people to prayer with these words:

God is most great, God is most great, God is most great, God is most great, I bear witness that there is no god but Allah, I bear witness that there is no god but Allah, I bear witness that Muhammad is the messenger of Allah, I bear witness that Muhammad is the messenger of Allah. Come to prayer, Come to prayer. Come to your good, Come to your good. God is most great, God is most great. There is no god but Allah.

Apart from prayer the mosque is also used as a place for teaching, for meetings and for quiet meditation.

Right The National Mosque at Kuala Lumpur, Malaysia, was opened in 1964 and has room for 8,000 worshippers.

Below Simplicity and grandeur are the hallmarks of mosque architecture. Details may vary greatly but the basic elements of a courtyard, a prayer-hall, facilities for ablution and usually a minaret, are always present in the larger mosques.

An Islamic Mosque

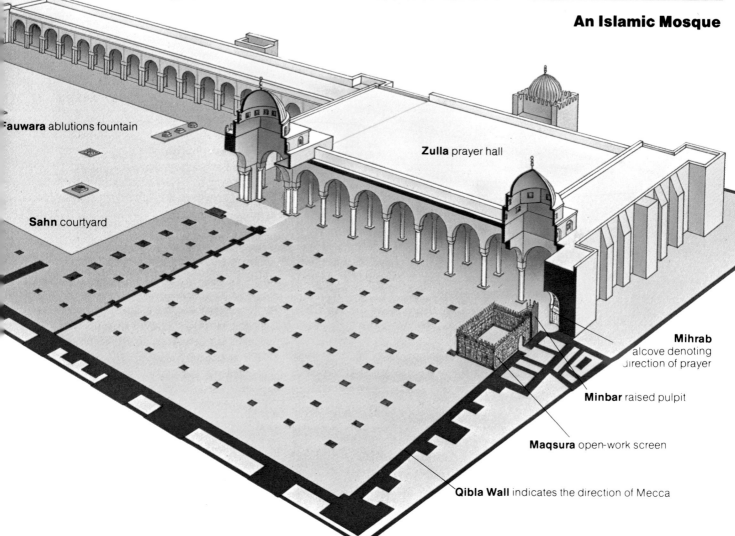

Fauwara ablutions fountain

Sahn courtyard

Zulla prayer hall

Mihrab alcove denoting direction of prayer

Minbar raised pulpit

Maqsura open-work screen

Qibla Wall indicates the direction of Mecca

Fasting and feasting

Right Congregational prayers, as seen here in the Cameroon, are an important part of both the Eid festivals.

Ramadan

Ramadan is the ninth month of the Muslim calendar and special because it was the month in which the Prophet first began to receive revelations from God. To remind them of this Muslims are supposed to fast for every one of the thirty days of Ramadan from dawn (when one can first tell a white thread from a black one) to sunset (when one can no longer do so). This means that they should not eat or drink anything at all, nor smoke, nor have sexual relations during this time.

During this month they should also say extra prayers and try to read the whole of the Qur'an. They should be particularly careful not to quarrel with friends and neighbours but should try to be particularly kind and helpful.

Fasting

Fasting in Ramadan teaches Muslims to value the good things God has provided for their enjoyment and to remember the sufferings of the poor and the hungry. Fasting is held to develop self-discipline and an attitude of generosity toward others.

All adult Muslims must keep the fast but very old people, the sick and women who are pregnant or feeding a baby are excused. Travellers may eat while they are on a journey but must make up the lost days later on.

Festival of Eid ul-Fitr

At the end of Ramadan comes the festival of Eid ul-Fitr. Muslims put on their best clothes and go to the mosque to pray together. Elaborate meals are prepared and served and visits made to relatives and

Right After the Eid ul-Fitr prayers at the mosque, a London family enjoys a special snack before going out to visit relatives.

friends. Children are given sweets and presents and new clothes to mark this happy occasion.

Festival of Eid ul-Adha

The other main festival of Islam is Eid ul-Adha, the festival of sacrifice, which celebrates Abraham's willingness to sacrifice his son Ishmael on God's orders. Through this festival Muslims record their willingness to sacrifice what they hold dear in order to carry out God's commands.

Eid ul-Adha occurs in the month of Dhul-hijja and coincides with the pilgrimage to Mecca. It is celebrated on the anniversary of the day when the Qur'an, God's revelation through Muhammad, was finally declared complete. Eid ul-Adha is also marked by the wearing of one's best clothes and prayer at the mosque. Muslims who can afford to do so sacrifice an animal and share the meat with their friends and relatives and the poor.

In Muslim countries these two festivals are celebrated as public holidays and shops, offices and schools are closed. Other Muslim festivals include the anniversary of the birth of the Prophet, the death of Ali's son Hussein at the battle of Kerbala and the anniversary of the Hijra (the Muslim New Year).

Meat prepared in a special way

Muslims may only eat meat that has been killed in a particular way. This involves the use of a sharp knife which must penetrate the inner part of the animal's neck. When the animal is being slaughtered the butcher should say *Bismillah* (in the name of God) to show that life is being taken only to provide for man's need for food. The blood is then drained from the carcase. Meat prepared in this way is called *halal* (permitted) meat.

Forbidden items

Muslims are also forbidden to eat the meat of the pig in any form. This not only means pork, bacon and ham but also any product containing pig fat (lard), such as biscuits or ice cream. For this reason Muslims need to know the ingredients of any item they buy while shopping.

Alcohol in any form is absolutely forbidden to Muslims. They should not provide it for their non-Muslim guests and should not take profits from it by selling it.

Right A fair outside the Al-Aksa mosque in Jerusalem marks the celebration of Eid ul-Fitr by local Arab children.

A pilgrimage to Mecca

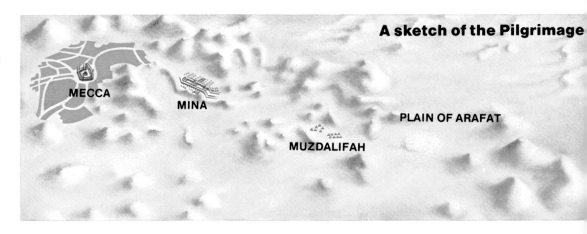

A sketch of the Pilgrimage

MECCA

MINA

MUZDALIFAH

PLAIN OF ARAFAT

Journey of a lifetime

Once in his or her lifetime a Muslim is obliged to undertake the *hajj* (the pilgrimage to Mecca). Only Muslims who can afford to do so are obliged to go. Muslims whose families would suffer by their absence should not go.

For most pilgrims their arrival in Arabia comes at the end of a long journey. They are reminded of the special purpose of their journey when they approach Mecca. Non-Muslims are forbidden to enter this area.

Simple dress

Male pilgrims wear only two seamless sheets of white cotton. This is because all of them, rich or poor, young or old, must look alike because they are alike in the sight of God. (There is no special costume for women but they must keep their faces unveiled.) During the pilgrimage the pilgrims are forbidden to

use soap or perfumes, to have sexual relations, to cut their hair or nails, to kill any living thing or even to pick wild flowers.

Seven stages

Upon reaching Mecca the pilgrim walks seven times round the Ka'aba. He then runs seven times between the hills of Safa and Marwa. This commemorates the incident when Hagar, the mother of Ishmael (ancestor of the Arab people), searched in the desert for water for her son and God caused the holy well of Zem-Zem to gush forth nearby.

On the eighth day of the month of Dhul-Hijjah the pilgrim stays overnight at Mina and then on the ninth day goes to the plain of Arafat, where Muhammad preached his last sermon. Here all the pilgrims gather and pray until nightfall. After staying overnight at Muzdalifah the pilgrim goes back to Mina to perform the ritual of stoning the devils.

Seven stones are thrown at three stone
pillars to commemorate Abraham's rejection
of Satan.

Then the pilgrim sacrifices an animal and
has his head shaved. After a final seven
circuits of the Ka'aba the rites of pilgrimage
are completed. Many pilgrims, however, go
on to visit Medina, where the Prophet
Muhammad is buried.

For fourteen centuries Muslims have
undertaken the hajj. It is the world's largest
annual spiritual gathering. Muslims from all
over the world remember their unity by
taking part in a common act of worship.

Daily life

Muslims in the developing world

Most Muslims live in the developing world. Perhaps because so many people think of them as Arab sheikhs (although five-sixths of all Muslims are not Arabs at all), they imagine them as nomads, living in the desert with herds of camels. Of course there are no deserts in the most populous Muslim countries, such as Indonesia and Bangladesh. And even in the Middle East Bedouin are only a tiny fraction of the population, perhaps 1%.

The cities of the developing world are growing rapidly. But the fact remains that the mass of the people in Muslim countries are villagers, working on the land or supplying people's daily needs through such crafts as carpentry, pottery and weaving. Families keep in close touch and relatives give each other help and advice.

Rural life

Villages in Muslim countries show the importance of Islam in the people's everyday life. The mosque is usually the largest building and often there is more than one. The idea that men and women should keep apart can be seen in the fact that only men go to the village guest-house or sit at the tables of the café, while women gather to talk at the well or in each other's houses.

Homes usually have strong doors and small windows and are built to face inwards onto a courtyard. Much of the household work is done in the courtyards and on the flat roofs. Family life is something to be kept private from outsiders. Visitors to a home will be shown into a guest-room and received by the men of the family, while the women stay in the background.

Muslims regard Islam as a complete way

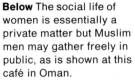

Below The social life of women is essentially a private matter but Muslim men may gather freely in public, as is shown at this café in Oman.

of life which involves directly religious practices such as prayer and also covers aspects of daily life such as food and drink.

Wealth

The laws and customs of Islam also affect how wealth can be earned and how it should be spent. Many passages in the Qur'an condemn the misuse of wealth. The Qur'an also sets out detailed rules for the inheritance of property. A Muslim is forbidden to deprive his family of a share in his estate. Muslims are also forbidden to lend money for interest (usury) or to gamble.

Death

Because Muslims believe in the resurrection of the body after death, they are always buried, never cremated. Before burial the body is washed (unless the believer has died in battle) and wrapped in a shroud. Then a funeral prayer is said. It is a duty laid upon all Muslims to see that believers have a proper funeral.

Women do not usually attend the burial but often visit the grave for years afterwards.

'Charity is incumbent on each person every day. Charity is assisting anyone, lifting provisions, saying a good word; every step one takes walking to prayer is charity, showing the way is charity.'

'Say part of your prayers at home so your houses do not become like graves.'

'There are two blessings which most people misuse—health and leisure.'

sayings of the Prophet Muhammad

Below The flat roofs and enclosed courtyards of this Tunisian city provide areas for women to work and relax, and symbolize the emphasis in Islam on the privacy of family life.

Childhood

Right Circumcision is an important ceremony in the life of Muslim boys. In some countries this is performed a few days after birth, but in Turkey it is done when boys are 7, 9, 11 or 13 years old. Special clothes are worn for the occasion.

Learning about Islam from birth

When Muslims become parents they have a special responsibility to ensure that their children grow up understanding their faith and what it requires of them. The very first thing a Muslim baby hears on coming into the world is the *shahadah* (the profession of faith)—'*I witness that there is no god but Allah and that Muhammad is the Prophet of Allah.*'

Muslim boys are circumcised, usually while they are still very young. There is nothing in the Qur'an that requires this but it has always been the custom among Muslims. The circumcision of a boy is an occasion for feasting and celebration.

Observing parents

Muslim children first learn about their religious duties by watching their parents, for instance at prayer. As they get older they are shown how to pray, taught to memorize parts of the Qur'an and encouraged to begin keeping the fast of Ramadan, at first for a day at a time and then for longer periods. By the time they are twelve or thirteen years old they should be able to carry out their religious duties like an adult.

Reciting the Qur'an

Learning to read and recite the Qur'an has always been an important part of education in Muslim countries. Nowadays schools in many Muslim countries make this part of the regular curriculum. In others and in many non-Muslim countries, Muslim children go to special classes after school instead. These classes are often held in the mosque and taught by the local *imam* (leader of prayers in a mosque).

Respect for older relatives

As teenagers Muslims are expected to work hard at school and to help around the house. Going out alone to parties and discos is discouraged, especially for girls. On the whole girls tend to be treated more strictly than boys. Teenagers of both sexes, however, are expected to show great respect towards their older relatives and to enjoy the company of their family.

'Be careful of your duty to Allah and be fair and just to your children.'

saying of the Prophet Muhammad

Right These people are members of one family in Iran who live together in the same village. Muslim families in the West are often widely scattered but still keep in very close touch with one another.

Below Traditional education was based almost solely on the Qur'an. Nowadays, as at this school in Pakistan, children must study other subjects as well.

Marriage

Arranged marriages

In Islam a happy family life is regarded as the foundation of a healthy society. The Qur'an encourages Muslims to marry and have children. It also emphasizes that sexual relationships outside marriage are always wrong.

Marriages between Muslims are often arranged by the parents and older relatives of the people involved. The prospective bride and groom have the right to refuse the person chosen for them and the marriage cannot go ahead if both partners do not agree.

In practice most young Muslims seem to trust their parents to make a good choice for them. Muslims believe that because parents know all about their children they will look for partners whose upbringing and personality will enable the couple to get on well together and also fit in with the life of the family as a whole.

Among Muslims marriage is thought of as more than a matter for two individuals. It involves all of the many relatives and therefore family opinion is a very important factor in bringing about marriages and encouraging them to last.

Rarely more than one wife

Muslim men are allowed to marry up to four wives but it is (and always has been) very rare for most ordinary Muslims to have more than one wife. Islamic law requires that each wife be treated equally in every respect. Few husbands can afford to support two wives for economic reasons (let alone four), so polygamous marriages are very much the exception rather than the rule.

Muslims do however think that it is good to be able to take a second wife if the first is unable to have children or becomes so ill that she needs someone to look after her and the household.

A wife's first duty

Looking after the home and family is a Muslim wife's first duty. She is not expecte to work outside the home to add to the family's income and indeed this is often frowned upon. Providing for the family is the main duty of the husband, though both parents bear responsibility for the upbringir of their children.

In most Muslim countries the family is a large group, consisting of many uncles and aunts and cousins, rather than the small parents-and-children group which is often thought of as the family in the West.

Members of this large, extended family network are expected to help each other in business matters or with domestic problems and to celebrate together at times of happiness. To be regarded as a fully adult member of this group a Muslim must really be married and have children of his or her own.

Divorce

Divorce is permitted in Islam but the Prophet said that it was the most hateful of all permitted things in the sight of God. Before Muslims get to the point of divorce they are encouraged to make every effort to reconcile their differences.

If divorce does occur the wife receives some money from her ex-husband and also takes all their household goods and furnitur But her maintenance then becomes the responsibility of her male relatives.

Right A Muslim bridegroom, veiled with flowers according to the custom of India and Pakistan, waits for his bride, accompanied by an imam.

Right A Bedouin wedding. The binding part of the ceremony is the signing and witnessing of a contract of marriage. The bride need not actually be present.

Women in Islam

Different duties
In Islam women and men have equal rights but different duties. Women have the same religious obligations as men, although they are excused attendance at the mosque on Fridays, so that they can be with their families.

Women have the same right as men to own property and to be educated, though in practice these rights have not always been respected by Muslim men. Islamic law also guarantees women a share in the property of their male relatives when they die, although they only receive half a man's portion of the inheritance. This is because Muslim men are bound to support their female relatives but Muslim women are not obliged to support their male relatives.

Caring for the family
Islam expects that men will chiefly be concerned with work and public affairs. The home and the care of the family are the main business of women. Indeed, one of the most famous of the Prophet's sayings was that paradise is to be found at the feet of your mother.

Working outside the home
Muslim women are allowed to work outside the home, providing this does not prevent them from taking proper care of their domestic duties. The sort of jobs that are favoured for Muslim women are caring occupations like nursing or teaching.

Women also do a vast amount of the agricultural work in villages and play a leading part in craft industries, especially textiles. Farm-work and carpet-weaving can however, usually be done at or near home and do not usually involve going away or working with strangers.

Guidelines for dress
The Qur'an requires men and women to behave modestly and decently towards one another. The Islamic ideal of modest behaviour sets out certain general guideline for how men and women should dress, but allows some variations to take account of different climates and customs.

Men should always be covered from the navel to the knees, even when swimming or taking a shower. They should not wear pure silk or gold or the special clothes associated

Right Women in Iran and other Muslim countries often reject Western dress in favour of traditional clothes.

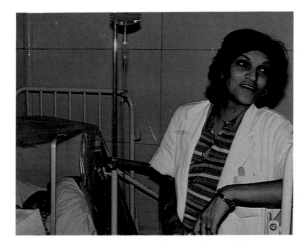

with other religions.

Women should cover their whole bodies except their faces and hands. Dresses should be loose and not reveal the shape of the body. Materials should not be transparent. When women are alone with close members of their family these rules need not be applied so strictly.

Great contrasts

The conditions of women's lives vary very greatly in different parts of the Muslim world, although everywhere they are changing because of Western influence, the growth of educational opportunities and the availability of birth-control. At present striking contrasts can be seen. In Syria and Iraq women are encouraged to work and take part in politics. In Saudi Arabia they are still not allowed to drive cars. The idea that women should live in *purdah* (seclusion), kept apart from men (except their male relatives) is still held to be important in many parts of the Muslim world.

The existence of the extended family means that women in purdah live not in isolation from one another but rather in their own women's world. However Muslim women who live in individual seclusion in non-Muslim countries far away from their relatives can often feel extremely isolated.

'Modesty is part of faith.'

'Visit the sick, feed the hungry and free the captives.'

'No one eats better food than that which he eats from the work of his own hands.'

sayings of the Prophet Muhammad

Sufis

Closer to God

Since the early days of Islam there have be Muslims who tried to become as close as possible to God. They were not content simply to follow the rules laid down in the Qur'an. Many of them believed that it contained secret meanings which could onl be understood by long study or thought.

Other Muslims tried to leave the everyda world far behind by going without food or sleep. These Muslims came to be called Su because they wore a rough woollen robe (*suf*) to show that they were not interested wealth or comfort. Over the years different brotherhoods of Sufis started, each followir the examples and teachings of a famous Su master of the past.

Each Sufi brotherhood had its own speci methods of reaching out towards God. Usually these methods were kept secret by members of the brotherhood who called them the *tariqa* (path). Some Sufis chant, some breathe rhythmically and others danc Perhaps the most famous are the Mevlevi dervishes (now to be found in Turkey) who whirl round and round.

The search

What the Sufis are searching for cannot easily be explained. Some have tried to explain it through poetry. Others, although they have not been interested in riches and power, have been greatly respected as wise and holy men.

Learned Muslims have sometimes oppos the influence of Sufis over other Muslims and have disapproved of such customs as praying at the tombs of Sufi holy men. But the influence of Sufis in North and West Africa, Pakistan and India remains strong.

Al-Ghazali

One of the most famous of all Sufis was Al-Ghazali (d.1111). He was a great scholar who became a brilliant teacher. Students travelled hundreds of miles to hear his lectures in Baghdad. One day he decided that learning from books was not enough to give him a full knowledge of God. So he became a Sufi for many years. But he always insisted that the mystic also needed to have a sound grasp of the Qur'an and the traditions of the Prophet—otherwise he might just become the victim of his own imagination.

Examples of Sufi writing

إلهي إن كنت عبدتك من خوف النار فأحرقني في النار، أو طمعاً في الجنة فحرمها علي، وإن كنت لا أعبدك إلا من أجلك فلا تحرمني مشاهدة وجهك.

O my Lord, if I worship Thee from fear of Hell, burn me in Hell, and if I worship Thee from hope of Paradise, exclude me thence, but if I worship Thee for Thine own sake then withhold not from me Thine Eternal Beauty.

فليتك تحلو والحياة مريرة   وليتك ترضى والأنام غضب

وليت الذي بيني وبينك عامر   وبيني وبين العالمين خراب

إذا صح منك الود فالكل هين   وكل الذي فوق التراب تراب

Would that you are sweet to me even if life is bitter, pleased with me even if all else is angry.
Would that what is between you and me is flourishing even if what is between me and all else is desolate.
If I secure your love, then all else is insignificant and all on earth is nought but earth.

Rabia Al-Adawiyya, a Sufi woman poet who died in Iraq, 801

35

Islamic art

Right This fireplace, in the Topkapi Palace, Istanbul, well illustrates the skill of Muslim craftsmen in ceramics and metalwork. It also shows the use of floral and calligraphic motifs.

Far right The Alhambra palace in Granada is one of the few surviving glories of seven centuries of Muslim rule in Spain. Its cool gardens, complex tile and mosaic decoration and delicately carved stucco work have inspired Western as well as Muslim artists and architects.

No human or animal figures

Islam has created its own styles of art and architecture. Because Muhammad preached against the worship of idols, Muslim artists were discouraged from making paintings or sculptures of people or animals. Instead they used designs based on flowers and plants or geometric patterns, like stars.

Calligraphy as decoration

Calligraphy, the art of beautiful writing, was especially praised and rewarded because it was a way of reminding Muslims of God's words in the Qur'an. Quotations from the Qur'an and the sayings of the Prophet, as well as proverbs and poetry, were used to decorate buildings, tiles, pottery, metalware and textiles. This tradition also shows the continuing power and importance of the Arabs' delight in their language.

Textiles as art

Textiles became especially important in Islamic art because wood was scarce in the Middle East so that woven items such as rugs, cushions and bags often took the place of beds, chairs and chests. They were particularly important to nomads, who could not carry much heavy furniture when they moved from place to place.

Beautiful gardens

Another form of art favoured by Muslim rulers was the creation of beautiful gardens. In the Qur'an paradise is often described as a garden. (The English word 'paradise' comes from a Persian word meaning 'garden'.) Cool, shady gardens with flowers and shrubs, pools and fountains were especially precious in the arid lands of the Middle East where Islam first spread.

Europeans learned many techniques, such as the use of pointed arches in buildings, from Muslim craftsmen. Pottery and carpets made by Muslim artists have been traded (and valued very highly) for centuries in non-Muslim countries all over the world.

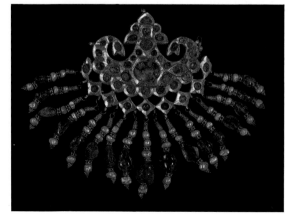

Scientific wonders

A search for knowledge
One of the most famous of the sayings of Muhammad was *'Look for knowledge, even as far away as China.'* Muslim rulers therefore encouraged scientists as well as artists. At Baghdad the Abbasids established a 'House of Wisdom' which was a great library and a translation centre where the writings of the ancient Greeks, Indians and Persians were translated into Arabic.

It is through these Arabic versions that European scholars first learned much of the scientific knowledge of the ancient world. Many modern English scientific terms (such as 'chemistry', 'zero' and 'rocket') come from Arabic. What are usually called Arabic numerals (1, 2, 3 and so on) were really invented in India, but it was Muslim scholars who worked out the full system of decimal calculation and passed it on to Europe, where it gradually replaced Roman numerals (I, II, III and so on).

Right A medieval treatise on the workings of the eye. Muslim scientists made important advances in optics and the treatment of eye diseases.

Right The need to find the direction of Mecca for the purposes of prayer gave Muslims an interest in astronomy from the earliest times. This astrolabe, made in the 17th century, was used to calculate the movements of stars and planets.

Far right This reconstruction of a pharmacy reminds us that traditional Muslim healers pioneered the use of many drugs and spread knowledge of their uses to the West. Many pharmacies sold a range of remedies and also made up prescriptions.

Drugs were carefully checked by inspectors who would call on a pharmacy at any time to make spot checks on the quality of drugs being sold. If a pharmacist was found to be cheating, the inspector could impose a heavy penalty such as a large fine or a beating.

Mathematics
Muslim scientists were especially interested in mathematics and astronomy. They practically invented algebra and trigonometry. These interests arose partly from the need to work out exactly the right times and direction for prayer. Muslims also had to plan their calendar and be able to work out how to share out inheritances according to the rules laid down in the Qur'an.

Medical research
In medicine Muslims concentrated on the use of drugs and herbs rather than surgery. They also knew about the importance of diet, climate and mental strain in affecting the health of patients. They became very expert in treating eye diseases which were very common in the Middle East. Muslims also set up public hospitals with trained, permanent staff, where young doctors could study and do research.

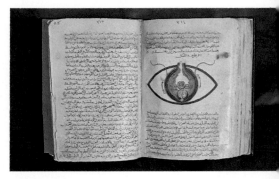

Amazing discoveries
Among the most famous Muslim scientists were Ibn al-Haytam (d.1039) who tried to find out how rainbows are caused, Ibn Sina (d.1037) who wrote a medical encyclopedia and described how epidemics spread, and al-Razi (d.925) who was the first scientist to tell the difference between smallpox and measles.

Astronomy and geography
Trade and pilgrimage encouraged Muslims to travel and in the deserts of the Middle East they often used the stars to help them find their way. Interest in astronomy and geography therefore had a practical value.

Al-Khwarizmi (d.846) was both a famous astronomer and a mathematician, as well as the compiler of the first Arabic atlas. Umar Khayyam (d.1123), who is better known in the West as a Sufi poet, was a court astronomer who devised a calendar as accurate as the one we use today.

Al-Biruni (d.1050) wrote a geography of India and guessed correctly that the Indus river valley must once have been a sea. Al-Idrisi (d.1166) compiled a famous atlas for Roger II, the Christian king of Italy.

'There is no disease for which Allah has not sent a cure.'

saying of the Prophet Muhamma

Modern Islam

Western colonization

Between the middle of the 18th century and the middle of the 20th century large parts of the Muslim world came under Western control. Many countries were conquered and ruled as colonies. Europeans at that time were entirely confident of the superiority of their technology, their military power, their religion, and indeed, their whole way of life.

One leader of a Muslim country even came to think that the Islamic way of life had made the people poor and backward. After the Ottoman Empire was defeated in the First World War the new leader of Turkey, Kemal Atatürk, brought in many changes in education and the laws. He even changed the calendar and the writing system and tried to make the people wear Western-style clothes. Most ordinary Turks, however, remained firm believers in traditional Muslim ways.

Achieving independence

Since the Second World War Muslim countries have regained their independence. As they have learned more about the West many Muslim leaders have come to believe that its way of life still has many problems and weaknesses, although most still admire its achievements in such fields as industry and medicine. Oil production and sales have given some influential Muslim countries (such as Saudi Arabia and Libya) great wealth. This has given them the opportunity to help poorer Muslim countries through foreign aid.

Far right Rising standards of education for women are widening opportunities for employment but, after marriage, the home and family should come first.

Right Even in modern Turkey traditional beliefs are a part of everyday life. This bumper-sticker calls on God's protection for a taxi-driver and his passengers.

Countries like Iran and Pakistan have turned against Western influences in recent years and called for a new commitment to Islamic ideals and ways. Even in countries where Western influences have been strong and long-established (as in Egypt and Tunisia) the trend towards strengthening Islamic traditions has also been seen.

In Malaysia students have organized ban on Western music and alcohol in the universities. These changes are not necessari a threat to Western countries and their way of life but they do show that Muslims wish their customs and traditions to be treated equally. Muslims increasingly feel able to face the future with confidence and faith in the eternal message of Allah and the teachin of his Prophet, Muhammad.

In Europe, North America and the West Indies Muslims have become permanent members of the community, organizing the own mosques and charities and in some cases their own schools. Although they live in non-Muslim societies they wish to keep their character as Muslims, wherever they are.

'It is charity for any Muslim who plants a tree or cultivates land which provides food for a bird, animal or man.'

saying of the Prophet Muhamma

Right Television studios in Kuwait. The different parts of the Muslim world are now being drawn closer together by modern mass communications.

Right A conference of representatives of Muslim countries. Muslims are increasingly acting together in economic and educational matters as well as in politics.

Further Information

Useful words—a glossary

Adhan announcement—the call to prayer.

Ahl al-Kitab the people of the book—i.e. Jews and Christians, who possess books of revelation.

Allah God.

Ansar helpers—the first converts in Medina, later used to denote all those who helped the Prophet in his campaigns.

Bismallah abbreviation of '*bismillah al-rahman, al-rahim*'—'in the name of God, the merciful, the compassionate'. A standard invocation used by Muslims before any significant act, task or journey.

Dervish member of Sufi religious order.

Dhikr remembering, mentioning—recitation of the names of God is a central feature of Sufi ritual; each order has its distinctive dhikr.

Dhimmi 'people of the covenant'—Jews or Christians living under Muslim rule. These protected classes were allowed to practise their own religion in return for payment of a poll-tax but were forbidden to exercise full civil rights.

Eid ul-Adha see **Id al-Adha**.

Eid ul-Fitr see **Id al-Fitr**.

Hadith saying, statement—a record of something said or done by the Prophet.

Hajj the pilgrimage to Mecca.

Hajji a person who has performed the hajj.

Halal permitted.

Haram sacred—sanctuary, holy territory. Term used to denote the environs of Mecca, Medina and Jerusalem.

Hijra the Prophet's departure from Mecca to Medina; variously translated as flight, emigration, exodus and breaking of ties. The Islamic calendar dates from this era.

Ibadah worship (plural—*ibadet*).

Id al-Adha (Eid ul-Adha) feast of sacrifices. Major festival of the Muslim calendar, celebrated on the 10th Dhul-Hijja, the day on which pilgrims make their sacrifices in the valley of Mina.

Id al-Fitr (Eid ul-Fitr) feast of the breaking. Festival to mark the end of the fast of Ramadan.

Ihram state of ritual purity assumed by pilgrims about to undertake the rites of hajj.

Imam he who stands at the front, leader of prayers in a mosque.

Iman faith, belief.

Islam submitting (to God), peace.

Jihad struggle—term used to denote both war in defence of the faith and the effort to overcome one's imperfections to become a better Muslim.

Ka'aba cube—the central shrine of Islam in Mecca.

Kafir unbeliever.

Khalifa successor—(Caliph) title assumed by heads of the Muslim community after the death of the Prophet.

Kiswa black cloth covering the Ka'aba.

Khutba sermon delivered in mosque at congregational prayer on Fridays.

Masjid a place of prostration, a mosque.

Mihrab recess in mosque wall denoting the direction of prayer.

Minbar pulpit from which the khutba is delivered.

Mu'adhdhin person who gives the call to prayer (muezzin).

Muslim a follower of Islam.

Nabi prophet.

Qibla the direction of prayer.

Qur'an (Koran) recitation—the sacred book of Islam.

Rak'a complete cycle of prescribed ritual movements performed during prayer.

Ramadan ninth month of the Muslim calendar. A period of dawn-to-dusk fasting.

Salat a ritual prayer, observed five times a day.

Saum a fast.

Shahada the profession of faith—*La ilaha illa'llah, Muhammad rasul Allah*—there is no god but Allah (and) Muhammad is the Prophet of Allah.

Shia party, fashion—name for historic subdivision of the Muslim community. Members of the various Shia traditions differ with regard to details of doctrine and ritual.

Sufi an Islamic mystic.

Sunna custom, practice—the words and deeds of the Prophet.

Sura a chapter of the Qur'an.

Tawhid the Oneness of God.

Umma the community of Muslims.

Wudu ablution performed before prayer.

Zakat alms, tax.

The Muslim calendar

Islam has its own calendar, which dates from the *Hegira* (*Hijra*) when the Prophet and his companions left Mecca for Medina (16 July 622). The year 1400 AH (Anno Hegirae) began at sunset on 19 November 1979.

The Muslim calendar was inaugurated by the second Caliph, Umar, who was faced with the practical problems of administering a rapidly expanding empire in which correspondence over long distances had to be accurately dated.

The Qur'an (10:5) decrees the use of lunar months and the Islamic year is therefore out of phase with the Gregorian calendar, which is based on the solar year. The lunar year is roughly 11 days shorter than the solar year and its months have, by convention, 29 and 30 days alternately. In relation to the Western system of reckoning therefore, the Muslim calendar moves 'backward' each year. This means that Muslim festivals fall at different times of the Western year and bear no fixed relation to the seasons.

To calculate conversions from one calendar to the other

a) The rule of thumb is that a Western (i.e. Gregorian) century equals 103 years according to the Muslim calendar. (And the year 1300 corresponded with 700 AH.)
b) A more exact formula is that where G = Gregorian year H = Hijra year.

$$G = H + 626 - \frac{H}{33}$$

$$H = G - 622 + \frac{G - 622}{32}$$

Books for further reading

Islam in General

The Religious Dimension: Islam—Riadh El-Droubie and Edward Hulmes (Longmans 1980)
Islam for Children—Ahmad von Denffer (The Islamic Foundation 1981)
Our Muslim Friends—Anne Farncombe (National Christian Education Council 1977)

History and Heritage

Muhammad and the Arab Empire—John Duckworth (Harrap 1974)
The Rise of Islam—Anton Powell (Longmans 1979)
Mohammed: His Times & Influence—Viola Bailey and Ella Wise (Chambers 1976)
The Buildings of Early Islam—Helen and Richard Leacroft (Hodder & Stoughton 1976)
The Moors—Gerald Hawting (Sampson Low 1978)
Muslim Spain—Duncan Townson (Cambridge University Press 1973)
The Spread of Islam—Michael Rogers (Phaidon 1976)

Muslims in Britain

Understanding your Muslim Neighbour—Muhammed and Maryam Iqbal (Lutterworth Educational 1976)
Nahda's Family—Madeleine Blakely (A & C Black 1977)
Shabnam's Day Out—Joan Solomon (Hamish Hamilton 1980)
Gifts and Almonds—Joan Solomon (Hamish Hamilton 1980)

Islam in the Modern World

Turkey—David Hotham (Macdonald Educational 1975)
Egypt—Michael von Haag (Macdonald Educational 1975)
Saudi Arabia—Eugene Gordon (Oak Tree Press Co. Ltd 1975)
Pakistan—Jon A. Teta (Oak Tree Press Co. Ltd 1972)
The Middle East—Maureen Abdullah (Macdonald Educational 1980)
The Arab World Today—Richard Tames (Kaye & Ward 1980)
The Middle East in the Twentieth Century—Richard I. Lawless (Batsford 1980)
Pakistani Village—Ailsa & Alan Scarsbrook (A & C Black 1979)
Arab Village—Roderic Dutton & John B. Free (A & C Black 1980)
The Oil States—W. B. Fisher (Batsford 1980)
The Muslim Guide—Mustafa Yusuf McDermott (The Islamic Foundation 1980)
Approaches to Islam—Richard Tames (John Murray 1982)

Places to visit

Here is a list of museums and art galleries which have interesting collections of items from the Muslim World. But it is advisable to make enquiries before you go as in some cases the exhibits may be in reserve collections or not normally on public display.

Major collections
Cambridge, Fitzwilliam Museum—
especially carpets, pottery.

Edinburgh, Royal Scottish Museum—
metalwork, armour, pottery and costume.

Glasgow, Burrell Collection, Camphill Museum—
carpets, pottery, metalwork.
Museum and Art Gallery—
weapons.

London, British Museum and King's Library—
comprehensive collection.
Science Museum—
scientific instruments.
Tower of London, New Armouries—
weapons, armour.
Victoria and Albert Museum—
comprehensive collection, notable for carpets.

Manchester Museum—
special collection of bows, weapons, armour.
Museum of the History of Science—
scientific instruments.

Sheffield Art Gallery—
pottery, paintings (Persia and Indian sub-continent).

Smaller collections
Aberdeen, University of Aberdeen Anthropological Museum—
some pottery.

Bath, Victoria Art Gallery—
little, uncatalogued, ceramics and some illuminated pages from manuscripts.

Batley, Bagshaw Museum—
some ceramics mainly of Multan (Pakistan).

Birmingham, City Museum and Art Gallery—
various.

Bradford, City Art Gallery—
uncatalogued collection from Indian subcontinent; available for loan by schools.

Bristol, City Museum and Art Gallery—
various exhibitions.

Cardiff, The Castle—
contains examples of 'Moorish' architecture.

Durham, Gulbenkian Museum of Oriental Art, University of Durham—
various.

Ipswich Museum—
carpets, weapons and domestic items.

London, Horniman Museum—
musical instruments.
The Most Venerable Order of St. John of Jerusalem Museum—
some armour and coins especially from the Holy Land.
National Army Museum—
mostly in store, especially from India.
Wallace Collection—
arms and armour.
Royal Artillery Museum, Rotunda Woolwich—
various weapons and armour.

Maidenhead, The Henry Reitlinger Bequest—
basically ceramic, a 'Persian Room'.

Merseyside County Museums, Departments of Antiquities and Ethnology—
mainly in store, manuscripts, pottery, metalwork, domestic items.

Oxford, Pitt Rivers Museum—
various examples of Muslim craftsmanship and some weapons.

Stoke-on-Trent, City Museum and Art Gallery—
good collection especially of Persian ceramics.

Index

Illustration credits
Key to position of illustrations:
(T) top, (C) centre,
(B) bottom, (R) right,
(L) left.

Artists
Aziz Al-Naib: 35
Nick Farmer: 8-9, 10, 12, 14
Tony Payne: 18, 20-21, 24

Photographic sources
Art and Architecture
   Collection: 12, 16, 23,
   36(B), 37(B)
Dr. Abdul-Haleem: 11
BPC Library/Chester
   Beatty Library, Dublin:
   15(T,B)
BPC Library/Wellcome
   Institute: 39
Daily Telegraph Colour
   Library: title page, 19,
   24, 25(T)
Sonia Halliday: 36, 37(T)
Robert Harding Picture
   Library: cover, 14, 18
   28-29, 34(B), 40(R)
Michael Holford: 38(L)
Geoff Howard: 31(T)
Alan Hutchison Library:
   contents page, 8(T,C),
   16(B), 17, 20, 21, 22(T)
   29(T), 32, 35, 41(T)
Alan Hutchison Library/
   From 'Pilgramage to
   Mecca' by Mohamed
   Amin: 25
MEPHA: 38(R)
Rex Features/Sipa Press:
   10, 41(B)
Richard Tames: endpapers,
   8(B), 22(B), 27, 28(T),
   30(L), 40(L)
John Topham Picture
   Library/Bente Fasmer:
   34(T)
John Topham Picture
   Library/Christine
   Osborne: 26, 30(R),
   31(B), 33T,B)
ZEFA: 13